An ARKFUL of ANIMAL stories

John Goodwin
Illustrated by Tina Macnaughton

LION
CHILDREN'S

Contents

For Robin   J.G.

For Richard Harris, 30 March 2006   T.M.

Text copyright © 2006 John Goodwin
Illustrations copyright © 2006 Tina Macnaughton
This edition copyright © 2006 Lion Hudson

The moral rights of the author and illustrator
have been asserted

A Lion Children's Book
an imprint of
Lion Hudson plc
Mayfield House, 256 Banbury Road,
Oxford OX2 7DH, England
www.lionhudson.com
ISBN-13: 978 0 7459 4922 2
ISBN-10: 0 7459 4922 3

First edition 2006
1 3 5 7 9 10 8 6 4 2 0

A catalogue record for this book is available
from the British Library

Typeset in 14/20 ITC Berkeley Oldstyle Bk BT
Printed and bound in China

Noah

When Noah heard God call to him, he was frightened.

'Don't be scared, Noah,' said God in a friendly voice. 'I've heard that you're a shipbuilder – is that true?'

'It is true,' answered Noah.

'Excellent,' said God. 'I want you to build the greatest ship in the world. This ark will have to be big enough to fit in two of every animal that breathes. Use all your skill, Noah, and ask all your family to help you. When the earth begins to flood, you and the animals must board the ark. Your lives will depend on it.'

9

The Hippo

Splish. Splash. Splash.

The rain was falling fast. It hadn't stopped for three whole days and nights. Hundreds of animals still needed to board the ark. Out of the jungle they cantered. Over land they scampered. In the air they flew. Chattering, squawking, trumpeting. Monkeys had tied creepers to the ark so crawly animals could climb along them up into safety without getting their feet wet.

But time was running out. Already the ark was floating and the land disappearing under the water.

'Help!' cried the animals left on land. 'It's too far for us to jump onto the ark. What can we do?'

Then they saw two hippos wallowing in the mud, having one last bath. They lifted their huge snouts and turned to look at the frightened animals. Lumbering forward, they held their bodies still in the water to make two giant stepping stones between the dry land and the ark.

'But I'm too scared,' whispered the armadillo.

One of the hippos lifted his head to give a friendly wink. Then they both began to snuffle with a gentle, muddy sort of sound.

The lions raised their heads and stepped forwards onto the first stepping stone.

The hippo's back was perfectly still and steady. With another step, the lions reached the second hippo, and with a third they stepped safely into the ark.

'It's our turn now,' whispered the camel. Two by two the animals on the land followed and carefully stepped from hippo to hippo into the ark.

'Thank you God,' sang the hippos in full-throated throttle. 'You have kept us calm in a time of crisis.'

The Giraffe

The giraffe's neck was amazingly long. It reached right up to the roof of the ark. But it didn't stop there. Oh no. It went through a round window and high into the air.

The giraffe didn't see the rest of the animals trying to sleep in the ark below her. Instead, her lips quivered and her teeth chomped. She wound her neck cleverly to reach the very highest leaves on the last unflooded trees. Chomp chomp chomp.

Way down below her, a tiny animal squeaked.

'What are you doing up there?' said the mouse in its loudest voice.

'Eating,' said the giraffe between mouthfuls.

'What else are you doing?' squeaked the mouse.

'Looking,' said the giraffe, not used to making conversation.

'What does it look like up there?' squeaked the mouse.

'There's water everywhere,' said the giraffe, trying to be more chatty.

'How deep is it?' squeaked the mouse.

'Deep enough to flood most of the earth. Soon it will cover even the tall mountains,' said the giraffe, who had never done so much talking.

'I wish I could see that,' said the mouse in a very sad squeak, trying to stand on tiny tiptoes.

The giraffe stopped chomping and lowered her neck into the ark.

'Climb up onto my neck, little one,' she said, 'and I'll show you.'

The mouse had never been so high nor seen so far.

She talked so much about her adventure that very soon lots of the other smaller animals one by one came to take a ride on the giraffe's neck.

'Thank you God,' said the giraffe, 'for all the new friends I've made. We all need to be friends for the adventure ahead.'

The Elephant

In the ark, the animals were all busy. They were brushing and sweeping. They were scrubbing and cleaning and polishing. Everyone was helping except the elephant. He was doing nothing at all.

Hour after hour he sat lazily on his own with his eyes half closed.

The animals were working all through the day. They were sifting and sorting. They were mending and fixing and carrying and shifting. But the elephant was still doing nothing at all. He sat lazily on the straw.

The turtle was tired and the skunk was shattered. The zebra was zapped and the wombat was whacked. Even the millipede was legless and the flea was fatigued.

'Oh dear,' they all groaned. 'Our brains are boggled and our bodies bedraggled.'

'The elephant's done nothing,' grumbled the gorilla.

'Lift your trunk, will you?' barked the seal.

But the elephant didn't move a single muscle.

Then night fell. The animals expected to fall asleep at once; but somehow they still felt busy inside.

'I'm thinking of home,' buzzed the bee.

'Me too,' mooed the cow.

That's when the elephant moved his trunk.

'Listen to my story,' he said. 'I've been writing it in my head all day.

'When the sun rises in the jungle it is the brightest and most beautiful thing in the world,' began the elephant. 'Trees shimmer and all

things glow in the greenness…'

The story carried the animals into the world of their dreams. His quiet words were soothing to their ears. Soon they were all fast asleep.

An elephant never forgets anything. God gave him a special gift as a storyteller, just as God gave every creature their own special talent.

The Lion

The blackness of the sky was lit up in a fierce storm as lightning flashed and thunder crashed. The rain poured down in buckets and everything was awash with water.

In a far corner of the ark, the lion had its paws over its eyes. A tiny flea usually liked to hide deep in the lion's mane, but at that moment it hopped out onto the tip of the lion's nose.

'Excuse me, mighty one,' whispered the flea.

'What is it?' replied the lion grumpily.

'Why do you have your paws over your eyes?' asked the flea.

'I'm trying to think,' said the lion.

'Are you scared of the lightning?' asked the flea.

'Oh no,' said the lion. 'I love lightning.'

Just then, a huge clap of thunder boomed in the heavens and the lion moved its paws to its ears.

The lion pretended it hadn't heard the question, so the flea hopped closer to its ear.

'Are you frightened of the thunder?' asked the flea.

'Oh no,' said the lion. 'I can roar more loudly than any thunder.'

At that moment, the ark was hit by a huge wave. It rocked and rolled and pitched and tossed. The lion started to tremble.

'Before you ask, little flea,' said the lion, 'I'm shivering because I'm cold.'

The flea looked into the lion's eye. It didn't believe the lion was telling the truth.

Nor did the rabbit or the gazelle or any of the animals that had gathered around.

The lion slowly lowered its paw and looked at them all.

'Oh dear,' it said. 'I'm supposed to be king of all animals. Wasn't I first to step onto the ark? Yet now I admit I'm very afraid.'

'We all are,' said the flea. 'It's always best to tell the truth. Then we can help one another.'

The Rattlesnake

Below deck it was very crowded. The ark was big, but fitting in all the hundreds and hundreds of different animals was still a bit of a squash.

One night the rattlesnake found himself squashed between the bison's bottom and an ape's armpit.

'This is seriously sniffy. I can't squirm or shake or slide or slither. I can't even sleep. And what's even worse is that I can't rattle at all. What good is a rattlesnake without a rattle?' it sighed. 'It's like having a camel without a hump or an elephant without a trunk.'

The rattlesnake slipped into a sulk. In the desert all the animals used to marvel at the way in which it rolled its Rs. 'RRRRRRRR!'

'I haven't even rolled my Rs since I've been on this stinky ship,' it sighed. 'I need room to rattle my body and roll my Rs. They go together. Like slide and slither.'

After another sleepless night, the rattlesnake was silently seething. Then, as the sun began to light the sky, the cockerel sang its morning song.

'COCK-A-DOODLE-DOO!'

The cricket clicked its heels, the hyena laughed, the swan hissed and the duck quacked.

'QUACK QUACK QUACK!'

'Such a surprise,' said the rattlesnake to itself.

'If there's room for them, then there's room for me.'

It made a tiny slither and tried to rattle. There was no sound at all.

The ape yawned and grunted and scratched itself. It made just enough room for a reasonable wriggle. The wriggle rose to a rattle as a roll of Rs rang out.

'RRRRRRR!'

The rattlesnake rejoiced as he rattled again.

It was a thank you rattle for the bright new day dawning.

The Monkeys

No onions. No turnips. And no carrots.

'But I love carrots,' neighed the horse. 'My belly will ache if I don't have carrots to munch.'

'My belly has been aching all day,' whined the weasel. 'There was nothing for me to eat at breakfast.'

'Me neither,' moaned the hedgehog, in a particularly prickly voice.

Only the owl had any wise words to say.

'Food is scarce. We must all share and save.'

'Share and save. Share and save.' The sheep bleated the words over and over again.

Late in the evening, the elephant finished telling one of his stories and let out a very loud trumpet. All the animals came running, crawling and skipping to a big wooden table in the centre of the ark. A huge cloth covered the table.

The sheep bleated, 'It's bananas, bananas. We can smell bananas.'

The elephant whipped away the cloth with a flick of his trunk.

To everyone's amazement, there were no

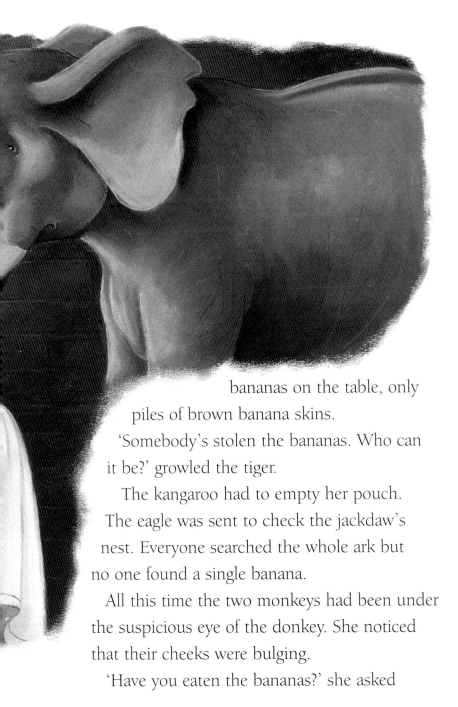

them. Both monkeys shook their heads slowly.

The owl flew up for a closer look.

'Their cheeks must be stuffed with bananas,' he hooted.

The monkeys looked at one another. They scratched their heads. They huddled close together and tried to swallow hard.

'Ooh, ooh, ooh, we've been found out,' they gibbered.

The elephant came and poked each of them with his trunk.

'You can't have eaten them all,' he said. 'Where are all the others?'

'On the roo-oo-oof,' sobbed the monkeys.

'Horumph,' said the elephant. 'In that case, you must go and fetch them back.'

bananas on the table, only piles of brown banana skins.

'Somebody's stolen the bananas. Who can it be?' growled the tiger.

The kangaroo had to empty her pouch. The eagle was sent to check the jackdaw's nest. Everyone searched the whole ark but no one found a single banana.

All this time the two monkeys had been under the suspicious eye of the donkey. She noticed that their cheeks were bulging.

'Have you eaten the bananas?' she asked

The Glow-worm

One night in the deepest room in the ark it was pitch black. It was so dark you couldn't see a flipper in front of your face or an elephant before your eyes. You couldn't see tails or claws or paws or beaks. Even the cat and tiger, whose eyes were used to seeing in the night, could hardly see anything but shapes and shadows.

In a little knothole in the timber, two glow-worms began to whisper together.

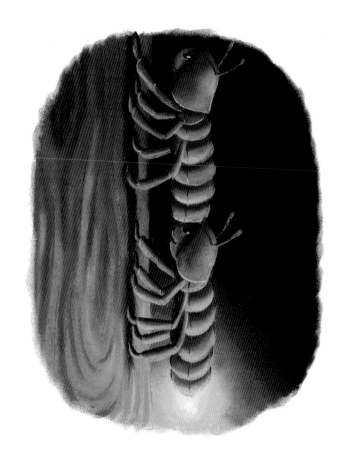

'Time for us to show ourselves,' they murmured.

'Where shall we go to?' they whispered.

'I'll crawl up onto the rafters,' said Mrs Glow-worm. 'You can fly up there first.'

'No no,' said Mr Glow-worm, 'I'll crawl up with you.'

'But it's so high,' said Mrs Glow-worm. 'It'll take us ages to crawl.'

'All the more reason to go together,' replied Mr Glow-worm.

Off they went together. Millimetre by millimetre they crawled, over the knots and splinters in the wooden planking. They climbed higher and higher until at last they found themselves on the very top rafter.

'Take a moment to catch your breath,' said Mr Glow-worm. 'Then… GLOW!'

A few seconds later Mrs Glow-worm began
to glow magnificently in the dark.

'It's a miracle,' murmured the marmot.

'Is it a star, high in the sky?' stammered the
starfish.

'It's the pole star,' said the polar bear
confidently.

'If only it were the moon,' howled the
wolf longingly.

As Mrs Glow-worm just went on glowing, the
animals began to talk longingly of the time when
the flood would be over. Then they could leave
the ark and live, not under a roof, but under the
sun and the moon and the stars.

The glow-worms had given the animals
hope in their darkest hour.

The Hare

The animals were fed up. They had been on the ark for days upon days upon days and still it hadn't stopped raining. The yak yawned and the sloth slumbered. The bat was bored and the donkey was drowsy.

'Are we nearly there yet?' squeaked the mouse.

No one answered.

'We must be nearly there,' squeaked the mouse. But her words fell into another long silence.

The mouse broke the silence again.

'Surely we're nearly there?' she squeaked.

'Shut up you stupid creature,' snapped the alligator, showing its teeth.

'Keep your squeaks to yourself, mouse,' clucked the duck.

'Don't cluck, duck,' roared the tiger.

'Don't roar, tiger,' howled the wolf. 'You're giving me a terrible headache.'

The argument went on and on. The duck clucked at the tiger, the tiger roared at the wolf. The wolf howled for want of something to do and soon the dog and the fox and the jackal joined in. The row lasted all day long and every animal was so sad.

The hare felt cross at all this nonsense. It tapped its foot… and then it remembered its favourite thumping rhythm.

'Thump thump thump, thump thump thump.'

Soon the rattlesnake joined in. 'Rattle rattle rattle, rattle rattle rattle.'

'Hum hum hum, hum hum hum,' went the bee.

'Caw caw caw, caw caw caw,' called the crow.

The animal band was growing. Soon the orang-utan drummed its chest, the elephant trumpeted, the hyena laughed and the bison bashed its feet. An animal orchestra was in full sound.

That's when the hare began to dance. It leaped and ran and jumped and capered. It was a skippereen sort of dance that everyone wanted to join in with.

Soon the sheep were shimmying, the
kangaroos were kicking and the porcupines
were pirouetting. Then the whole ark began
to rock.

25

The Raven

'Listen,' cawed the raven.

'I can't hear anything,' purred the cat, quietly licking its paws.

'Exactly,' cawed the raven. 'You can't hear anything.'

'I can't be doing with your raven riddles,' purred the cat, preening its whiskers and flicking its tail.

'Hearing nothing means it's stopped raining,' cawed the raven loudly.

The animals peered out of porthole windows. Someone drew back a latch and opened the hatch. Paws and toes climbed up steps. Heads and bodies, tails and toes appeared on deck. It was true. The rain had stopped.

'Hooray,' cried the parrot.

'Hurrah,' shouted the monkey.

'Hallelujah,' sang one and all.

Three days went by. There was no more rain.

The flood water began to drop. The ark crunched against something solid: land at last.

26

'Raven,' called Noah. 'I want you here.'

'You are the clever one, Raven,' said Noah, holding the bird on the back of his hand. 'Seek out the craggy mountain tops. When you return we'll know you have found dry land.'

The bird's jet-black body soared into the sky but a strong wind blew it sideways. On it flew, struggling hard.

'Of course I'll find land, of course I'll find land,' it cawed.

But even though it flew and flew, it saw nothing but brown flood water. Its body was tired and its heart was heavy.

Then at last the raven saw a small cluster of rocks rising out of the water.

'They will make a perfect nesting site,' it cawed as it flew down to them.

It rested a while on the rocks and gathered its strength. It pecked tiny green shoots growing out of a crevice in the rock.

'Soon other birds will leave the ark,' it cawed. 'Soon my mate will come to join me.'

Time passed and the raven grew lonely. No other birds came to join it. But still it cawed and waited and cawed again, hoping that it would not be alone for ever.

The Dove

There was sadness on the ark. Long days passed and the raven didn't return. Still everyone scanned the skies and the silvery surface of the sea for any sign of the returning bird. But it was all for nothing.

Every crumb of food had been eaten. Every animal was feeling low. Something had to be done. But what?

Noah looked round carefully at all the birds perched in the rafters. 'Another bird will have to do what the raven could not,' he said.

Should he choose the flamingo to fly off next, or would it be the golden eagle that took to the skies? What about the swift or the swallow, the gull or the heron?

Noah chose the dove. He whispered a prayer and set it free. Every animal prayed for its safe return.

Time plodded by. Still the skies were empty.

'If the raven failed, what chance has the dove?' whispered the sloth. 'It's rather plump for such a long journey.'

The hawk fixed its beady eye on the horizon.

Suddenly it flapped its wings and screeched out loud.

'What can you see? What have you spotted?' everyone squealed.

'A tiny dot high in the sky,' cried the hawk.

As the dot grew into a small winged shape, a huge double rainbow formed in the heavens.

It spanned the sky in glorious brilliant colour.
Each band was a dazzle. Under its arch the dove
returned with an olive twig in its beak.

'Look,' said Noah. 'God has given us a
signal of peace in the new world that is
about to begin. Let us give thanks
for his almighty blessing.'

29

Other titles from Lion Hudson

The Lion Book of Five-Minute Bible Stories *Lois Rock & Richard Johnson*

Lion Children's Favourites *30 Bible Stories and Prayers*

Dinner in the Lions' Den *Bob Hartman & Tim Raglin*